nF421414

A Brief History of Ancient Egypt

Timelines of History 4th Grade
Children's Ancient History

In this book, we're going to talk about a brief history of Ancient Egypt. So, let's get right to it!

The Egyptian civilization was around for almost 3,000 years. The unification of Upper Egypt and Lower Egypt in 3100 BC marks the beginning of the Ancient Egyptian civilization. Egypt's monuments, art, religious rituals, and early hieroglyphic writing have captured the imaginations of archaeologists and historians around the world. In fact, research about Egypt has created a field of study exclusive to it, called Egyptology.

Historians use two different ways to organize Egypt's history in order to study it.

Ptolemy VI relief
Temple of Kom Ombo

DYNASTIES

Throughout the course of Egyptian history, different powerful families took control of the government. They kept control by passing the power of rule from generation to generation within their family line. The king or chief ruler of Egypt was called the pharaoh. If you include the Ptolemaic Dynasty that was formed by the Greeks, over the almost 3,000-year span of Egyptian civilization, there were over 30 different dynasties.

KINGDOMS AND PERIODS

Another way of organizing Egyptian history is by dividing it into the different kingdoms and periods. The three kingdoms are labeled as the Old Kingdom, the Middle Kingdom, and the New Kingdom. In between the ending of one kingdom and the beginning of another, there were periods of transition called "intermediate" periods.

Pyramids of Egypt

The following timeline gives a brief snapshot of the history of ancient Egypt.

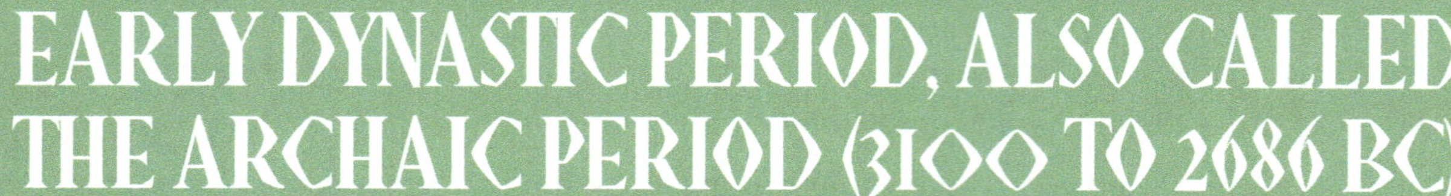

EARLY DYNASTIC PERIOD, ALSO CALLED THE ARCHAIC PERIOD (3100 TO 2686 BC)

First And Second Dynasties

Prior to 3100 BC, Egypt had two different kingdoms, Upper Egypt and Lower Egypt. King Menes joined these two kingdoms into one unified Egypt. He established a capital city near the Nile River's delta. Eventually, this capital was known as Memphis. It grew into a huge city that was the major influence in Egyptian society in the subsequent period of Old Kingdom.

Upper Egypt

During this time, the Egyptians developed the belief that their rulers were like gods. The ruler was identified with the god Horus who was the very powerful god of the sky depicted with the head of a falcon. The earliest picture writing, called hieroglyphics, dates from this era as well.

During the Early Dynastic Period, most of the citizens of Egypt farmed to earn their living. They had learned to farm grains, chiefly wheat as well as barley, and these crops formed the basis of their economy.

Their agricultural cycle was based on the yearly flooding of the Nile River. The river provided the needed water and fertile soil. They sowed the fields after the flooding was past and harvested them before the dry cycle began.

OLD KINGDOM (2686 TO 2181 BC)

Third Through Sixth

Pharaohs. King Djoser commissioned Imhotep, a well-known priest and architect, to create a monument for him for the afterlife. The result of this amazing achievement was the Step-Pyramid, which was located close to the capital of Memphis in the city of Saqqara. It was the beginning of a period of pyramid building that reached its golden age with the creation of the Great Pyramid located at Giza, outside Cairo.

Step pyramid of King Djoser at Saqqara

The Great Pyramid was built for the Pharaoh Khufu and later was proclaimed by historians as one of the Seven Wonders built during ancient civilizations. Two other enormous pyramids were built in the city of Giza for the pharaohs that came after Khufu—Khafra and Menkaura.

During the first part of the period of Old Kingdom, the third and fourth dynasties, Egypt enjoyed a peaceful time filled with prosperity. The government was stable and the people agreed with the principle that the pharaohs held all the power. There were no serious threats from foreign countries and Egypt's military campaigns added to its prosperity. During the fifth and sixth dynasties, things shifted however.

Pharaoh Throne Hall

Pyramid building was expensive and had gotten out of control with more and more elaborate pyramids. The wealth of the government was depleted so the pharaohs became weakened in power. Noblemen and priests who worshipped the sun god Ra, also called Re, began to gain power. By the end of the sixth dynasty, Egypt was in chaos.

FIRST INTERMEDIATE PERIOD (2181 TO 2055 BC)

Seventh Through Tenth Dynasties

There was a quick succession of rulers from the city of Memphis until around 2160 BC. By now, the central government was so weakened that it almost didn't exist. A civil war between governors of the provinces broke out. Seizing the opportunity because of the weakened government, the Bedouins, who were nomadic tribes of Arab descent, invaded and the country was decaying with both famine as well as rampant diseases.

Arab water-carrier girls in Egypt

As the chaos continued, two different kingdoms emerged. Throughout the ninth and tenth dynasties, there were 17 rulers. They were based in the city of Heracleopolis and they ruled the lands of Middle Egypt between the cities of Memphis and Thebes.

Meanwhile, another group of rulers emerged in the city of Thebes. In 2055 BC, a Theban prince by the name of Mentuhotep overthrew the rulers in power and reunited the country once more. This was the beginning of the eleventh dynasty. This event marked the beginning of the Middle Kingdom period.

THE TEMPLE OF QUEEN HATSHEPSUT
IN LUXOR, EGYPT

Mentuhotep III

MIDDLE KINGDOM
(2055 TO 1786 BC)

Eleventh And Twelfth Dynasties

At the end of the eleventh dynasty, the last of the Mentuhotep family, Mentuhotep IV was assassinated. The throne was passed to his "right-hand man," Amenemhet I, who had been the pharaoh's vizier.

menemhet I established a new capital city at It-towy, which was south of the previous capital of Memphis. The city of Thebes continued to be a powerful religious hub. During this time, Egypt thrived once again. To avoid future chaos, the pharaohs made each of their successors into co-regents. In that way, the future rulers could learn the process of ruling.

Luxor Temple is a temple complex
located in the city of Luxor
(ancient Thebes)

During this time, Egypt colonized Nubia and expelled the Bedouins from the land. They began their building projects again and built fortresses for the military and quarries for mining as well as pyramid tombs. This period ended with the twelfth dynasty, which was ruled by Queen Sobekneferu. She was the first woman to hold that position.

SECOND INTERMEDIATE PERIOD (1786 TO 1567 BC)

Thirteenth Through Seventeenth Dynasties

By the thirteenth dynasty, once again, the government was in chaos. Numerous kings tried to gain and unify the power seats with no success. As a result, the official court and government was moved to the city of Thebes. Another dynasty, the fourteenth, began in the city of Xois located in the delta. These two dynasties were ruling at the same time.

LUXOR

HYKSOS

A family of foreign rulers called the Hyksos came to Egypt around 1650 BC and gained control, forming the fifteenth dynasty. Although they were foreigners, they kept many of the Egyptian traditions in place. Historians are unsure as to whether the sixteenth dynasty was made up of Theban rulers or Hyksos rulers.

However, they do know that the seventeenth dynasty was occurring at the same time in Thebes. Conflict erupted between the two groups. The native Thebans started a war against the foreign Hyksos group and forced them out of the country at the end of this period.

The Ramesseum at Thebes

Ahmose-Meritamun's
inner coffin

NEW KINGDOM
(1567 TO 1085 BC)

Eighteenth Through Twentieth Dynasties

Egypt was united once again under Pharaoh Ahmose I during the eighteenth dynasty. Egypt was becoming an empire and its influence stretched from Nubia all the way to Asia's Euphrates River. This dynasty was known for its powerful Pharaohs, such as Amenhotep I, Thutmose I, and Amenhotep III.

Under the reign of Amenhotep III, Egyptian civilization reached its peak of wealth, power, culture, and art. The role of women became more dominant as well with the rule of Queen Hatshepsut who rose to rule first as regent for Thutmose III, her young stepson, and eventually became pharaoh.

PROCESSIONAL COLONNADE OF
AMENHOTEP III AT DAWN

Akhenaton

During the latter part of the eighteenth dynasty, Amenhotep IV took the throne. He disbanded the worship of the god Amon-Re and the other gods and goddesses and forced the worship of one god, the sun-god Aton.

The pharaoh renamed himself Akhenaton and along with his queen Nefertiti built a new capital located in Middle Egypt after his new name. After Akhenaton died, the religious practices went back to their old ways.

The nineteenth and twentieth dynasties were ruled by the pharaohs called Ramses, so this was called the Ramesside period. According to the Old Testament of the Bible, the exodus of the Israelites more than likely occurred during the rule of Ramses II, sometime between 1304 to 1237 BC.

NEFERTITI

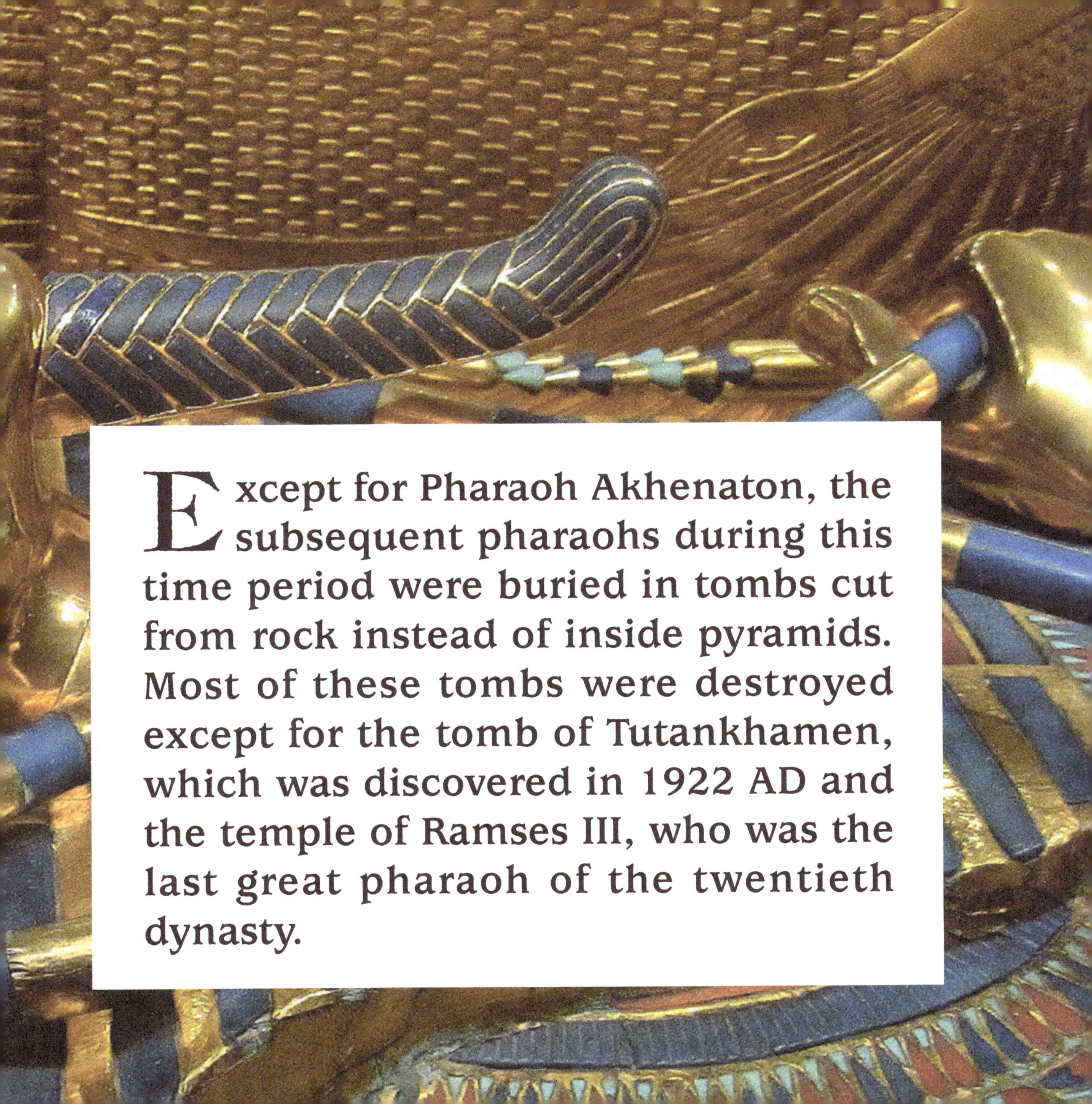

Except for Pharaoh Akhenaton, the subsequent pharaohs during this time period were buried in tombs cut from rock instead of inside pyramids. Most of these tombs were destroyed except for the tomb of Tutankhamen, which was discovered in 1922 AD and the temple of Ramses III, who was the last great pharaoh of the twentieth dynasty.

THIRD INTERMEDIATE PERIOD
(1085 TO 664 BC)

Twenty-First Through Twenty-Fourth Dynasties

During this period, the New Kingdom ended and Egypt was once again divided. The empire became weaker and the Assyrians conquered Egypt. Beginning with the twenty-first dynasty, this period went through the twenty-fourth dynasty.

Assyrian soldiers

PERSIAN SOLDIER

LATE PERIOD
(664 TO 332 BC)

Twenty-Fifth Through Thirtieth Dynasties

From the twenty-fifth dynasty to the thirtieth dynasty, the Assyrians left Egypt and the local powers regained control once again until the Persians took over in 525 BC. They ruled until 332 BC when Alexander the Great and his Grecian armies conquered the Egyptian empire.

Alexander built the global city of Alexandria, which eventually became the new capital. In 305 BC, Alexander's General, Ptolemy I ruled as pharaoh. The Ptolemaic Dynasty was the last one and ruled from 305-30 BC. The very last pharaoh was the famous Cleopatra VII who died in 30 BC.

Alexander the Great Founding Alexandria

Now you know more about the history and timeline of the kingdoms and dynasties of Ancient Egypt. You can find more Ancient History books from Baby Professor by searching the website of your favorite book retailer.

Visit

BABY PROFESSOR
EDUCATION KIDS

www.BabyProfessorBooks.com

to download Free Baby Professor eBooks
and view our catalog of new and exciting
Children's Books